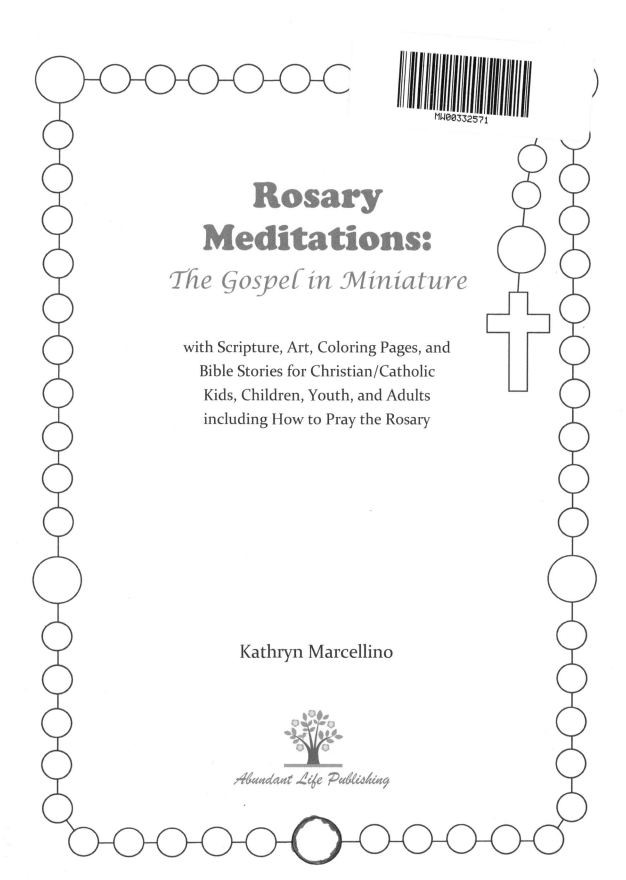

Rosary Meditations:

The Gospel in Miniature

with Scripture, Art, Coloring Pages, and
Bible Stories for Christian/Catholic
Kids, Children, Youth, and Adults
including How to Pray the Rosary

Kathryn Marcellino

Abundant Life Publishing

Rosary Meditations: The Gospel in Miniature
with Scripture, Art, Coloring Pages, and Bible Stories
for Christian/Catholic Kids, Children, Youth, and Adults
including How to Pray the Rosary

by Kathryn Marcellino

Cover design, coloring book illustrations, and graphic design by Kathryn Marcellino.
The art masterpieces used for each mystery are from the public domain.
The cover painting (inside the box) is *Madonna of the Rosary* by Bartolome Esteban Murillo (1600s).
A special thank you to Joan M. Lehman for help in editing this book.

Abundant Life Publishing
PO Box 3753
Modesto, CA 95352
email: km@abundantlifepublishing.com
www.AbundantLifePublishing.com

13-digit ISBN: 978-0-945272-56-4

Printed in the U.S.A.

≈≈∧∧∩∩≈

Dedication

This book is dedicated to Our Lord and Savior Jesus Christ and our Blessed Mother Mary.
It was written for the young and young at heart especially for my children and grandchildren.

≈≈∧∧∩∩≈

About the Author: Kathryn Marcellino is the mother of five children and a growing number of grandchildren. She is a member of the Catholic Church and the Secular Order of Discalced Carmelites (OCDS), as well as being a spiritual director with training in spiritual direction from the Diocese of Stockton, CA, School of Ministries and The Mercy Center in Burlingame, CA. She founded and maintains a website on spiritual direction where she offers a free e-mail newsletter and an online course entitled "Seeking Union with God" (www.CatholicSpiritualDirection.org). Kathryn is the author of *How to Pray the Rosary as a Pathway to Contemplation*. She is also a freelance artist and graphic designer (www.MarcellinoDesign.com).

Table of Contents

Prayers of the Rosary

The Sign of the Cross
In the name of the Father, and of the Son and of the Holy Spirit. Amen.

The Apostles' Creed
I believe in God, the Father almighty, Creator of heaven and earth, and in Jesus Christ, his only Son, our Lord, who was conceived by the Holy Spirit, born of the Virgin Mary, suffered under Pontius Pilate, was crucified, died and was buried; he descended into hell; on the third day he rose again from the dead; he ascended into heaven, and is seated at the right hand of God the Father almighty; from there he will come to judge the living and the dead. I believe in the Holy Spirit, the holy Catholic Church, the communion of saints, the forgiveness of sins, the resurrection of the body, and life everlasting. Amen.

The Our Father
Our Father, who art in heaven, hallowed be thy name; thy kingdom come; thy will be done on earth as it is in heaven. Give us this day our daily bread; and forgive us our trespasses as we forgive those who trespass against us; and lead us not into temptation, but deliver us from evil. Amen.

The Hail Mary
Hail Mary, full of grace, the Lord is with you; blessed are you among women, and blessed is the fruit of your womb, Jesus. Holy Mary, Mother of God, pray for us sinners now and at the hour of our death. Amen.

The Glory Be (The Doxology)
Glory be to the Father, the Son, and the Holy Spirit; as it was in the beginning, is now, and ever shall be, world without end. Amen.

Optional Fatima Prayer
Oh my Jesus, forgive us our sins, save us from the fires of hell; lead all souls to heaven, especially those most in need of Your Mercy.

The Hail Holy Queen (Salve Regina)
Hail, holy Queen, mother of mercy, our life, our sweetness, and our hope. To you we cry, poor banished children of Eve; to you we send up our sighs, mourning and weeping in this valley of tears. Turn, then, most gracious advocate, your eyes of mercy toward us; and after this, our exile, show unto us the blessed fruit of your womb, Jesus. O clement, O loving, O sweet virgin Mary. Amen.

Optional Ending Prayers
Pray for us, O holy Mother of God that we may be made worthy of the promises of Christ. Let us pray. O God, whose Only Begotten Son, by his life, death, and resurrection, has purchased for us the rewards of eternal life, grant, we beseech thee, that meditating upon these mysteries of the most holy Rosary of the Blessed Virgin Mary, we may imitate what they contain and obtain what they promise, through the same Christ Our Lord. Amen.

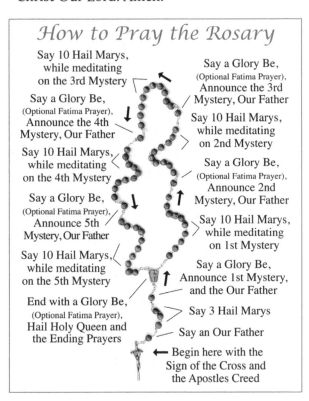

How to Pray the Rosary

Say 10 Hail Marys, while meditating on the 3rd Mystery

Say a Glory Be, (Optional Fatima Prayer), Announce the 4th Mystery, Our Father

Say 10 Hail Marys, while meditating on the 4th Mystery

Say a Glory Be, (Optional Fatima Prayer), Announce 5th Mystery, Our Father

Say 10 Hail Marys, while meditating on the 5th Mystery

End with a Glory Be, (Optional Fatima Prayer), Hail Holy Queen and the Ending Prayers

Say a Glory Be, (Optional Fatima Prayer), Announce the 3rd Mystery, Our Father

Say 10 Hail Marys, while meditating on 2nd Mystery

Say a Glory Be, (Optional Fatima Prayer), Announce 2nd Mystery, Our Father

Say 10 Hail Marys, while meditating on 1st Mystery

Say a Glory Be, Announce 1st Mystery, and the Our Father

Say 3 Hail Marys

Say an Our Father

Begin here with the Sign of the Cross and the Apostles Creed

The Rosary is a Bible-based prayer. It begins with the Apostles' Creed, which is a summary of the beliefs of the Catholic faith. The mysteries of the rosary, many taken directly from the Gospels, highlight important events in the lives of Jesus, and his mother Mary. The Our Father is the prayer that Jesus taught the disciples to pray (Matthew 6:5-13). The prayer, Hail Mary, also mainly comes from Scripture. The Hail Mary begins with the words of the Angel Gabriel's announcement to Mary that she had been chosen to be the mother of the Jesus. "Hail, full of grace, the Lord is with you!" (Luke 1:38) The second sentence of the Hail Mary is from Mary's cousin, Elizabeth, who exclaimed to Mary, "Blessed are you among women, and blessed is the fruit of your womb!" (Luke 1:41-42).

The idea of honoring Mary is also Scriptural as seen in Luke 1:46-48: "And Mary said, 'My soul magnifies the Lord, and my spirit rejoices in God my Savior, for he has regarded the low estate of his handmaiden. For behold, henceforth all generations will call me blessed..." Jesus honors his mother and so should we as she is our mother also.

The rosary is prayed by saying vocal prayers while meditating on the mysteries. Thinking about the mysteries helps us to get to know Jesus and Mary better and to love them more. At Fatima, Portugal, in 1917, Mary appeared to three children and asked them to, "Pray the rosary every day." Lucia said, "My impression is that Our Lady wanted to give ordinary people, who might not know how to pray, this simple method of getting closer to God." (www.ewtn.com)

Even children can learn to pray the rosary and meditate on the mysteries. At Fatima Mary taught seven-year-old Jacinta how to meditate on the mysteries of the rosary by forming images of the mysteries in her mind as she prayed the Hail Marys. Small children are capable of understanding a lot. To meditate means to think about and ponder. The *Catechism of the Catholic Church*

(#2708) says, "Meditation engages thought, imagination, emotion, and desire. This mobilization of faculties is necessary in order to deepen our convictions of faith, prompt the conversion of our heart, and strengthen our will to follow Christ. Christian prayer tries above all to meditate on the mysteries of Christ, as in *Lectio Divina* or the rosary. This form of prayerful reflection is of great value, but Christian prayer should go further: to the knowledge of the love of the Lord Jesus, to union with him."

The Old Testament: Our Jewish Roots

To really understand the Gospel of Jesus Christ, it helps to realize that God made the whole universe and everything in it including us. The Bible's Old Testament is a history of God's work from creation to the time of Jesus. The first people he made were Adam and Eve and from them came all the other people on earth. God put them in a beautiful garden called Paradise where there was no sickness, sin, or death. There he told them not to eat the fruit of one tree in the garden.

Before God made humans he made angels. The *Catechism of the Catholic Church #366*, talks about good angels and our Guardian Angel: "From its beginning until death, human life is surrounded by their watchful care and intercession. Beside each believer stands an angel as protector and shepherd leading him to life."

Some of the angels, however, rejected God and became bad angels called devils. Devils hate God and people and now tempt people to sin. One devil, Satan (disguised as a snake) tempted Eve to disobey God. She listened to Satan and decided to disobey God; she ate the forbidden fruit and gave some to Adam to eat, and he disobeyed God too. This is called Original Sin because it was the first time humans sinned. (Sin is when we do something we know is wrong against God's will, or don't do something we can and know we should through our own free will.) When it is about a serious matter we can lose God's grace in our soul. This is called a serious or mortal sin. But God will forgive us if we are truly sorry. If we really love God, we will do what God wants. God is all good. He created us and loves us. He wants us to love him in return so we can be happy with him forever.

"And we have seen and testify that the Father has sent his Son as the Savior of the world. Whoever confesses that Jesus is the Son of God, God abides in him, and he in God. So we know and believe the love God has for us. God is love, and he who abides in love abides in God, and God abides in him." (1 John 4:14-16)

God knows all things and is all powerful and only wanted what was best for Adam and Eve (and all of us), but Adam and Eve thought they knew more than God regarding what was best for them and disobeyed God. The result of their sin was that they had to leave Paradise and were subject to sickness and death. They lost other gifts for themselves and also for us, who are their descendents who have inherited the effects of their original sin, such as being subject to sickness, death, and temptation.

God created the world and it was good, but through sin evil entered the world. The good news is that God promised Adam and Eve that he would send a Savior to save the world from sin and to reopen the gates of heaven that were closed by Adam and Eve's sin. This Savior is called the Messiah or Jesus Christ.

Over time Adam and Eve had many descendents until there were many people in the world. The Old Testament records their story. God also made a covenant with some of their descendents who came to be known as the Chosen People, Israelites, or Jewish people. God sent prophets to teach them and to prepare them for the coming of the promised Messiah. Jesus would come to save people from Original Sin, and all the sins committed in the world, so that people would have the chance once again to restore their place with God and also to go to heaven some day.

Who is Jesus Christ?

Jesus is the God the Son, the second person of the Blessed Trinity (Father, Son and Holy Spirit), who became a man through being born of Mary. He is the long-awaited Messiah and Savior of the whole world. The *Catechism of the Catholic Church* #479-483 says, "At the time appointed by God, the only Son of the Father, the eternal Word, that is, the Word and substantial image of the Father, became incarnate; without losing his divine nature he assumed human nature. Jesus Christ is true God and true man, in the unity of his divine person; for this reason he is the one and only mediator between God and men. Jesus Christ possesses two natures, one divine and the other human, not confused, but united in the one person of God's son. Christ, being true God and true man, has a human intellect and will, perfectly attuned and subject to his divine intellect and divine will, which he has in common with the Father and the Holy Spirit. The Incarnation is therefore the mystery of the wonderful union of the divine and human natures in the one person of the Word."

The Bible says in John 3:16, "For God so loved the world that he gave his only Son, that whoever believes in him should not perish but have eternal life."

The Rosary, the Gospel in Miniature

The Rosary is sometimes called the Gospel in miniature because the mysteries encompass the main events in the lives of Jesus Christ and Mary, his mother.

Preparation for Prayer

Decide on a good time and place for prayer in order to have minimal outer distractions. Before beginning to pray we should take a moment to recollect ourselves, which means putting ourselves in the presence of God as best as we can mentally and emotionally. We should try to set aside all our other concerns for the prayer time or make them part of your prayer by placing them all in God's hands. "Cast all your anxieties on him, for he cares about you. " (1 Peter 5:7)

Meditating on the Mysteries

Prayer is a communication between God and us. While saying the vocal prayers of the rosary we meditate (think about or dwell on) on the mystery for each decade. The mysteries are events from the life of Jesus and Mary. The Joyful Mysteries are about Jesus' conception, birth, and childhood, and are said on Mondays and Saturdays. The Luminous Mysteries are about Jesus' public ministry, and are said on Thursdays. The Sorrowful Mysteries are about Jesus' suffering and death, and are said on Tuesdays and Fridays. The Glorious Mysteries are about events after Jesus' death, and are said on Sundays and Wednesdays. (Exceptions are that the Joyful Mysteries are said on the Sundays of the Christmas Season and the Sorrowful Mysteries on the Sundays of Lent.)

Praying the Rosary

For each mystery, this book has an art masterpiece, a bible story for children, an illustration/coloring page, and a bible passage and/or other writings for reflection and to help better understand and visualize the event.

One way to pray the rosary is to say the beginning six prayers of the rosary while paying attention to the meaning of the words. We begin the rosary by saying The Apostle's Creed which contains the basic truths of our faith. Then we say the Our Father, which is the prayer Jesus taught us to pray. Following this we say three Hail Marys in honor of Mary and to ask her to pray for us. Then we say the Glory Be, which is a prayer of praise to God.

Next we announce the first mystery, for example, "the First Joyful Mystery is The Annunciation." At this time we could change our focus from thinking about the meaning of the words of the prayers to thinking about the meaning of the mystery for that decade. So while we say the Our Father, 10 Hail Marys, and Glory Be for the decade, we may meditate on the mystery just announced. (See page 4 for the prayers and instructions on praying the rosary.)

Some ways to meditate on the mysteries are to imagine ourselves as actually present at the event. What did Jesus and Mary do and say? What might they have felt? What would we think and feel if we were one of the actual witnesses or participants? What does God wish to communicate to us? The mysteries contain important lessons. God is always near and enlightens us in prayer as we open our hearts and minds to him.

The Family Rosary

Some ideas for praying as a family are to set a usual time that is best for everyone, perhaps right before the children's bedtime. It's a good idea for each child to have their own rosary. One idea is to wait until it's dark to say the rosary and then turn off most or all of the lights so the children will be less distracted. Perhaps let the children take turns lighting a special candle and blowing it out at the end.

Another idea is to let the children take turns leading the decades if they are old enough and to let them each add their own intentions before beginning the rosary. If saying the whole rosary is too difficult, one idea is to say one decade and then allowed them to go to bed or leave after that if they choose.

The goal is to encourage them to pray and to associate prayer with a positive experience and not with punishment or negative interactions. If they see the lights off, the candle burning, and everyone else praying, this often pulls them in to want to be included. Children and teenagers often have serious concerns. Offering to say the rosary for their special intentions may encourage them to want to be a part of the family rosary. (Bribing is not recommended.)

The main goal of parenting is to love the children, to teach them about God and how to follow Jesus, and to give them a positive, happy childhood. In this way they will more likely want to love God and others, be good, and want to go to heaven someday, which is ultimately what really matters for all of eternity as everything else is passing away.

1st Joyful Mystery: The Annunciation

The Annunciation by Nicolas Poussin, 1657

Bible Story: Mary was a very special young Jewish woman who lived about 2,000 years ago. From an early age Mary learned about God and how to be good. When Mary was about 14 years old and engaged to be married to St. Joseph, the Angel Gabriel appeared to her and said, "Hail Mary, full of grace the Lord is with you." The angel told her that she was highly favored because God had chosen her to be the mother of Jesus, the Son of God. The angel told Mary to name her son, "Jesus", which means Savior. Jesus came to save the world from their sins and open the gates of heaven once again. He also told her that this would happen through the Holy Spirit. Mary said, "Behold, I am handmaid of the Lord. Let it be to me according to your word."

Bible Reading:

Luke 1:26-38

[26] In the sixth month the angel Gabriel was sent from God to a city of Galilee named Nazareth, [27] to a virgin betrothed to a man whose name was Joseph, of the house of David; and the virgin's name was Mary. [28] And he came to her and said, "Hail, full of grace, the Lord is with you!" [29] But she was greatly troubled at the saying, and considered in her mind what sort of greeting this might be. [30] And the angel said to her, "Do not be afraid, Mary, for you have found favor with God. [31] And behold, you will conceive in your womb and bear a son, and you shall call his name Jesus. [32] He will be great, and will be called the Son of the Most High; and the Lord God will give to him the throne of his father David, [33] and he will reign over the house of Jacob for ever; and of his kingdom there will be no end." [34] And Mary said to the angel, "How shall this be, since I have no husband?" [35] And the angel said to her, "The Holy Spirit will come upon you, and the power of the Most High will overshadow you; therefore the child to be born will be called holy, the Son of God. [36] And behold, your kinswoman Elizabeth in her old age has also conceived a son; and this is the sixth month with her who was called barren. [37] For with God nothing will be impossible." [38] And Mary said, "Behold, I am the handmaid of the Lord; let it be to me according to your word."

Reflection: Jesus Christ is the Son of God, the second Person of the Blessed Trinity, from all of eternity. He became human like us through being born of the Virgin Mary while remaining God. Mary loved God very much and said yes to God. Do you love God and say yes to God like Mary did?

Visitation by Domenico Ghirlandaio, 1491

Bible Story: When the Angel Gabriel appeared to Mary, he also told her that her cousin, Elizabeth, was going to have a baby in about three months. Mary went to visit Elizabeth and stayed with her for about three months. It was a miracle that Elizabeth was going to have a baby because she was very old, but her baby was a special baby. He would be called John the Baptist, because he was going to help prepare people for the coming of Jesus. When Mary got to Elizabeth's house, Elizabeth said that the baby, John, inside her womb leapt for joy at the presence of Jesus in the womb of Mary. According to tradition, grace was given to St. John the Baptist at that very moment. Elizabeth said to Mary, "Blessed are you among women, and blessed is the fruit of your womb," which is the second sentence of the Hail Mary prayer.

Bible Reading:

 ## Luke 1:39-45, 57-60

39 In those days Mary arose and went with haste into the hill country, to a city of Judah, 40 and she entered the house of Zechariah and greeted Elizabeth. 41 And when Elizabeth heard the greeting of Mary, the babe leaped in her womb; and Elizabeth was filled with the Holy Spirit 42 and she exclaimed with a loud cry, "Blessed are you among women, and blessed is the fruit of your womb! 43 And why is this granted me, that the mother of my Lord should come to me? 44 For behold, when the voice of your greeting came to my ears, the babe in my womb leaped for joy. 45 And blessed is she who believed that there would be a fulfillment of what was spoken to her from the Lord." ... 57 Now the time came for Elizabeth to be delivered, and she gave birth to a son. 58 And her neighbors and kinsfolk heard that the Lord had shown great mercy to her, and they rejoiced with her. 59 And on the eighth day they came to circumcise the child; and they would have named him Zechariah after his father, 60 but his mother said, "Not so; he shall be called John."

Reflection: Mary loved God and she loved people. Jesus said to love others as we love ourselves and to treat others as we would have them treat us. How can we best love ourselves and others? Do we forgive others as we want to be forgiven? Do we return good for evil and pray for those who persecute us? Do we help the less fortunate? Jesus said that loving God above all things and loving others as we love ourselves are the two most important things for us to do.

11

The Nativity by Lorenzo Lotto. 1523

Bible Story: When it was almost time for baby Jesus to be born, Mary and Joseph, her husband, had to travel to Bethlehem. When they got to the town, there were no rooms left for them except a stable or cave for animals. While there, Mary's time came and she had the baby, Jesus, and laid him in a manger. We call the day Jesus was born Christmas day. While Jesus and his family were still at the stable, angels appeared to shepherds in the field nearby who were taking care of their sheep. The angels sang praises to God and told the shepherds that a Savior had been born who is Christ the Lord. So they hurried to see baby Jesus who was lying in the manger.

Reflection: Jesus while remaining the Son of God was born as a human being like us. He said he would be with us always, even until the end of the world. How can we love and visit Jesus today?

Bible Reading:

 *Luke 2:1-16*

1 In those days a decree went out from Caesar Augustus that all the world should be enrolled. 2 This was the first enrollment, when Quirinius was governor of Syria. 3 And all went to be enrolled, each to his own city. 4 And Joseph also went up from Galilee, from the city of Nazareth, to Judea, to the city of David, which is called Bethlehem, because he was of the house and lineage of David, 5 to be enrolled with Mary, his betrothed, who was with child. 6 And while they were there, the time came for her to be delivered. 7 And she gave birth to her first-born son and wrapped him in swaddling cloths, and laid him in a manger, because there was no place for them in the inn. 8 And in that region there were shepherds out in the field, keeping watch over their flock by night. 9 And an angel of the Lord appeared to them, and the glory of the Lord shone around them, and they were filled with fear. 10 And the angel said to them, "Be not afraid; for behold, I bring you good news of a great joy which will come to all the people; 11 for to you is born this day in the city of David a Savior, who is Christ the Lord. 12 And this will be a sign for you: you will find a babe wrapped in swaddling cloths and lying in a manger." 13 And suddenly there was with the angel a multitude of the heavenly host praising God and saying, 14 "Glory to God in the highest, and on earth peace among men with whom he is pleased!" 15 When the angels went away from them into heaven, the shepherds said to one another, "Let us go over to Bethlehem and see this thing that has happened, which the Lord has made known to us." 16 And they went with haste, and found Mary and Joseph, and the babe lying in a manger.

Presentation in the Temple
by Giotto di Bondone, 1304-1306

Bible Story: Forty days after Jesus was born, Joseph and Mary took Jesus to the Temple in Jerusalem for Mary's ritual purification after childbirth and to present Jesus as Mary's firstborn in obedience to the Law of Moses. While they were there, the Holy Spirit told Simeon, who was righteous and devout, that the baby, Jesus, was the Messiah. Simeon took Jesus in his arms and gave praise and thanks to God for allowing him to see the Savior (also called the Messiah) before he died. Simeon told Mary that her child was set for the falling and rising of many in Israel, that a sword would pierce through her soul, and that she would have much to suffer. Anna, an elderly prophetess was also in the Temple offering prayers and thanks to God for Jesus. She told everyone there about Jesus and his role in the redemption of Israel.

Bible Reading:

 *Luke 2:22-33*

²² And when the time came for their purification according to the law of Moses, they brought him up to Jerusalem to present him to the Lord ²³ (as it is written in the law of the Lord, "Every male that opens the womb shall be called holy to the Lord") ²⁴ and to offer a sacrifice according to what is said in the law of the Lord, "a pair of turtledoves, or two young pigeons." ²⁵ Now there was a man in Jerusalem, whose name was Simeon, and this man was righteous and devout, looking for the consolation of Israel, and the Holy Spirit was upon him. ²⁶ And it had been revealed to him by the Holy Spirit that he should not see death before he had seen the Lord's Christ. ²⁷ And inspired by the Spirit he came into the temple; and when the parents brought in the child Jesus, to do for him according to the custom of the law, ²⁸ he took him up in his arms and blessed God and said, ²⁹ "Lord, now lettest thou thy servant depart in peace, according to thy word; ³⁰ for mine eyes have seen thy salvation ³¹ which thou hast prepared in the presence of all peoples, ³² a light for revelation to the Gentiles, and for glory to thy people Israel." ³³ And his father and his mother marveled at what was said about him.

Reflection: Jesus, Mary, and Joseph obeyed the laws of Moses of their time. The Bible says in Romans 13:1-2, "Let every person be subject to the governing authorities. For there is no authority except from God, and those that exist have been instituted by God. Therefore he who resists the authorities resists what God has appointed, and those who resist will incur judgment." Many people today do not obey authorities. Do you obey those in authority over you unless they ask you to sin?

Finding in the Temple, wayside shrine, Austria

Bible Story: **When Jesus was 12 years old, he went with his parents to Jerusalem to celebrate the feast of the Passover. On the way back home, Mary and his step-father, Joseph, couldn't find Jesus among their relatives and friends. They looked for him for three days and finally found him in the Temple talking to the teachers who were all amazed about how much he knew about God and the things of God. Mary and Joseph asked Jesus why he had stayed behind as they were worried about him. He said, "Did you not know that I must be in my Father's house?" His parents didn't understand what he meant. Even though Jesus was God, he was obedient to his parents. His mother, Mary, thought about all these things kept them in her heart.**

Bible Reading:

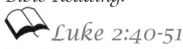
Luke 2:40-51

[40] And the child grew and became strong, filled with wisdom; and the favor of God was upon him. [41] Now his parents went to Jerusalem every year at the feast of the Passover. [42] And when he was twelve years old, they went up according to custom; [43] and when the feast was ended, as they were returning, the boy Jesus stayed behind in Jerusalem. His parents did not know it, [44] but supposing him to be in the company they went a day's journey, and they sought him among their kinsfolk and acquaintances; [45] and when they did not find him, they returned to Jerusalem, seeking him. [46] After three days they found him in the temple, sitting among the teachers, listening to them and asking them questions; [47] and all who heard him were amazed at his understanding and his answers. [48] And when they saw him they were astonished; and his mother said to him, "Son, why have you treated us so? Behold, your father and I have been looking for you anxiously." [49] And he said to them, "How is it that you sought me? Did you not know that I must be in my Father's house?" [50] And they did not understand the saying which he spoke to them. [51] And he went down with them and came to Nazareth, and was obedient to them; and his mother kept all these things in her heart.

Reflection: When Jesus talks about his Father's house, he is speaking of his Father in heaven. Jesus calls us to become God's children and to call God our Father. "Our justification comes from the grace of God. Grace is *favor*, the free and undeserved help that God gives us to respond to his call to become children of God, adoptive sons, partakers of the divine nature and of eternal life." (*Catechism of the Catholic Church* #1996) Even as a child, Jesus answered his Father in heaven's call to teach people about God. Are you responding to God's callings in your life?

The Baptism of Christ
by Bartolomé Esteban Murillo, 1655

Bible Story: When Jesus grew up, it was time for him to leave his parents' house and teach the people. John the Baptist went before Jesus and preached a "baptism of repentance for the forgiveness of sins" with water. John called people to repent and be sorry for their sins and to stop sinning. John the Baptist told the people he was not the Christ and his mission was to get things ready for Jesus. When Jesus went down to the Jordan River, he asked John to baptize him. When John baptized Jesus, the heavens opened up and the Holy Spirit descended upon Jesus like a dove. A voice from heaven said, "Thou art my beloved Son; with thee I am well pleased."

Bible Reading:

Mark 1: 1-5, 7-15

1 The beginning of the gospel of Jesus Christ, the Son of God. 2 As it is written in Isaiah the prophet, "Behold, I send my messenger before thy face, who shall prepare thy way; 3 the voice of one crying in the wilderness: Prepare the way of the Lord, make his paths straight." 4 John the baptizer appeared in the wilderness, preaching a baptism of repentance for the forgiveness of sins. 5 And there went out to him all the country of Judea, and all the people of Jerusalem; and they were baptized by him in the river Jordan, confessing their sins.... 7 And he preached, saying, "After me comes he who is mightier than I, the thong of whose sandals I am not worthy to stoop down and untie. 8 I have baptized you with water; but he will baptize you with the Holy Spirit." 9 In those days Jesus came from Nazareth of Galilee and was baptized by John in the Jordan. 10 And when he came up out of the water, immediately he saw the heavens opened and the Spirit descending upon him like a dove; 11 and a voice came from heaven, "Thou art my beloved Son; with thee I am well pleased." 12 The Spirit immediately drove him out into the wilderness. 13 And he was in the wilderness forty days, tempted by Satan; and he was with the wild beasts; and the angels ministered to him. 14 Now after John was arrested, Jesus came into Galilee, preaching the gospel of God, 15 and saying, "The time is fulfilled, and the kingdom of God is at hand; repent, and believe in the gospel."

Reflection: Jesus was baptized, and the Bible says we should be also. "And Peter said..., 'Repent, and be baptized every one of you in the name of Jesus Christ for the forgiveness of your sins; and you shall receive the gift of the Holy Spirit.'"(Acts: 2-38) The Most Holy Trinity gives the baptized sanctifying grace and our sins are wiped away in baptism. Have you repented of your sins? Would you like to be baptized if you haven't been?

A 14th century Fresco from the
Visoki Dečani monastery in Metohia (Kosovo)

Bible Story: Jesus and his disciples were attending a wedding when the party ran out of wine. Jesus' mother, Mary, told Jesus, "They have no wine." Even though Jesus said it was not yet time to reveal his power to the world, Mary told the servants, "Do whatever he tells you." Jesus ordered the servants to fill the big jars with water and to take some of it to the head waiter. After tasting it, the head waiter congratulated the bridegroom on saving the best wine for last. This was the first miracle or sign that Jesus did that revealed Jesus' "glory" as the Son of God, and his disciples believed in him. Jesus performed many other miracles later.

Bible Reading:

 John 2: 1-12

1 On the third day there was a marriage at Cana in Galilee, and the mother of Jesus was there; 2 Jesus also was invited to the marriage, with his disciples. 3 When the wine failed, the mother of Jesus said to him, "They have no wine." 4 And Jesus said to her, "O woman, what have you to do with me? My hour has not yet come." 5 His mother said to the servants, "Do whatever he tells you." 6 Now six stone jars were standing there, for the Jewish rites of purification, each holding twenty or thirty gallons. 7 Jesus said to them, "Fill the jars with water." And they filled them up to the brim. 8 He said to them, "Now draw some out, and take it to the steward of the feast." So they took it. 9 When the steward of the feast tasted the water now become wine, and did not know where it came from (though the servants who had drawn the water knew), the steward of the feast called the bridegroom 10 and said to him, "Every man serves the good wine first; and when men have drunk freely, then the poor wine; but you have kept the good wine until now." 11 This, the first of his signs, Jesus did at Cana in Galilee, and manifested his glory; and his disciples believed in him. 12 After this he went down to Capernaum, with his mother and his brothers and his disciples; and there they stayed for a few days.

Reflection: Jesus showed that he was God by performing miracles. Mary did not tell Jesus what or how to do things, but just told him the problem and put it into his hands. This is a good lesson for us because God knows best. Do you do whatever God tells you and pray for acceptance of God's way of doing things? Are you patient while waiting for God to answer?

The Sermon on the Mount by Carl Heinrich Bloch

Bible Story: When Jesus was about 30 years old, he went out to teach the people and proclaim the Gospel. (Gospel means "good news.") The good news was that the kingdom of God was at hand. Jesus said to believe in God and ask for the forgiveness of sins. Jesus taught people what God wanted them to do and how they should live. He told them to have faith in him, to stop sinning, to obey God's commandments, and to love God and their neighbor. He worked many miracles to show people that he was God, including healing the sick and raising the dead.

Bible Reading:

Mark 1:15

15 ... and saying, "The time is fulfilled, and the kingdom of God is at hand; repent, and believe in the gospel."

Mark 2: 3-12

3 And they came, bringing to him a paralytic carried by four men. 4 And when they could not get near him because of the crowd, they removed the roof above him; and when they had made an opening, they let down the pallet on which the paralytic lay. 5 And when Jesus saw their faith, he said to the paralytic, "My son, your sins are forgiven." 6 Now some of the scribes were sitting there, questioning in their hearts, 7 "Why does this man speak thus? It is blasphemy! Who can forgive sins but God alone?" 8 And immediately Jesus, perceiving in his spirit that they thus questioned within themselves, said to them, "Why do you question thus in your hearts? 9 Which is easier, to say to the paralytic, `Your sins are forgiven,' or to say, `Rise, take up your pallet and walk?' 10 But that you may know that the Son of man has authority on earth to forgive sins," he said to the paralytic, 11 "I say to you, rise, take up your pallet and go home." 12 And he rose, and immediately took up the pallet and went out before them all; so that they were all amazed and glorified God, saying, "We never saw anything like this!"

Luke 7:47-48

47 Therefore I tell you, her sins, which are many, are forgiven, for she loved much; but he who is forgiven little, loves little." 48 And he said to her, "Your sins are forgiven."

John 20:22-23

22 And when he had said this, he breathed on them, and said to them, "Receive the Holy Spirit. 23 If you forgive the sins of any, they are forgiven; if you retain the sins of any, they are retained."

Reflection: We need to study, especially the Bible and the *Catechism of the Catholic Church* (www.vatican.va), to know and to understand what God requires of us. We also need to accept Jesus and do what he taught to be in the kingdom of God. Do you study the teachings of Jesus? Do you do what Jesus asks us to do?

The Transfiguration, *Raphael, 1516-1520*

Bible Story: Jesus went up a high mountain with Peter, James, and John. While they were there he was changed so that his face shone like the sun and his clothes became as white as light. The apostles saw Moses and Elijah talking to him. From a bright cloud a voice said, "This is my beloved Son, with whom I am well pleased, listen to him." The apostles were filled with awe and fell down on the ground, and when they looked up again they only saw Jesus there. On the way back down the mountain, Jesus told the three apostles not to tell anyone what they had seen until he had risen from the dead. This was God's way to tell the apostles to listen to Jesus, his Son, who is above even the law of Moses and the prophets like Elijah.

Bible Reading:

Matthew 17:1-13

[1] And after six days Jesus took with him Peter and James and John his brother, and led them up a high mountain apart. [2] And he was transfigured before them, and his face shone like the sun, and his garments became white as light. [3] And behold, there appeared to them Moses and Elijah, talking with him. [4] And Peter said to Jesus, "Lord, it is well that we are here; if you wish, I will make three booths here, one for you and one for Moses and one for Elijah." [5] He was still speaking, when lo, a bright cloud overshadowed them, and a voice from the cloud said, "This is my beloved Son, with whom I am well pleased; listen to him." [6] When the disciples heard this, they fell on their faces, and were filled with awe. [7] But Jesus came and touched them, saying, "Rise, and have no fear." [8] And when they lifted up their eyes, they saw no one but Jesus only. [9] And as they were coming down the mountain, Jesus commanded them, "Tell no one the vision, until the Son of man is raised from the dead." [10] And the disciples asked him, "Then why do the scribes say that first Elijah must come?" [11] He replied, "Elijah does come, and he is to restore all things; [12] but I tell you that Elijah has already come, and they did not know him, but did to him whatever they pleased. So also the Son of man will suffer at their hands." [13] Then the disciples understood that he was speaking to them of John the Baptist.

Reflection: Jesus revealed his glory to Peter, James, and John. He allowed them to see that he was not just an ordinary human, but the Son of God. Do you realize that Jesus is really God who became a man to save us from our sins, to give us grace, to teach us the truth, and help us to get to heaven? Do you put God first in your life?

The Last Supper by Leonardo da Vinci, 1495-1498

Bible reading:

Matthew 26:17-20, 26-30

¹⁷ Now on the first day of Unleavened Bread the disciples came to Jesus, saying, "Where will you have us prepare for you to eat the passover?" ¹⁸ He said, "Go into the city to a certain one, and say to him, `The Teacher says, My time is at hand; I will keep the passover at your house with my disciples.' " ¹⁹ And the disciples did as Jesus had directed them, and they prepared the passover. ²⁰ When it was evening, he sat at table with the twelve disciples;... ²⁶ Now as they were eating, Jesus took bread, and blessed, and broke it, and gave it to the disciples and said, "Take, eat; this is my body." ²⁷ And he took a cup, and when he had given thanks he gave it to them, saying, "Drink of it, all of you; ²⁸ for this is my blood of the covenant, which is poured out for many for the forgiveness of sins. ²⁹ I tell you I shall not drink again of this fruit of the vine until that day when I drink it new with you in my Father's kingdom." ³⁰ And when they had sung a hymn, they went out to the Mount of Olives.

Reflection: At Mass, the priest is following Jesus' instructions to "do this in remembrance of me." (Luke 22:19) During the words of consecration, the water and wine is changed into the body and blood of Jesus. When we receive Holy Communion we are in reality receiving Jesus (body, blood, soul, and divinity) under the appearances of bread and wine. This is a miracle at each Mass. Are you faithful in attending Mass and receiving communion?

Bible Story: On the night before Jesus died on the cross, he had his last supper with his apostles. It was on the Jewish feast of the Passover when a lamb was slain and eaten in remembrance of when God and Moses brought the Jewish people out of slavery from the land of Egypt to the Promised Land. At Mass, Jesus is called the "Lamb of God who takes away the sins of the world." (John 1:29) In the Old Testament, animal sacrifices were offered for sins, but couldn't take away sins. However, the sacrifice that Jesus made by dying on the cross made up for all the sins of the entire world including our sins. Jesus, our Savior, the Lamb of God, gave his apostles himself to eat under the appearances of bread and wine, which he said were his body and blood. After Jesus' perfect sacrifice of himself, there didn't need to be any more animal sacrifices in the Temple. When Jesus said to the apostles, "Do this in remembrance of me," he started the sacrament of the Eucharist or Holy Communion. Jesus desires to be united with us and be in communion with us. He loves us and wants us to love him in return and to love one another.

Jesus praying to God the Father in Gethsemane
by Heinrich Hofmann, 1890

Bible Story: Right after eating his last supper with the apostles, Jesus went to the Garden of Gethsemane to pray. He was suffering so much that "his sweat became like great drops of blood falling upon the ground." (Luke 22:44) He was with Peter, James, and John whom he asked to stay awake for an hour and pray. Jesus knew that he would soon be dying on the cross to make up for all the sins of the world. He prayed three times to his Father in heaven to not have to suffer so much, but he wanted God the Father's will to be done and not his own will. Each time he checked and found the apostles asleep. An angel came from heaven to help strengthen Jesus. Today the "holy hour" devotion comes from Jesus' request to his apostles to spend an hour with him in prayer.

(www.therealpresence.org/eucharst/pea/holyhour.html)

Bible Reading:

 *Matthew 26:36-46*

36 Then Jesus went with them to a place called Gethsemane, and he said to his disciples, "Sit here, while I go yonder and pray." 37 And taking with him Peter and the two sons of Zebedee, he began to be sorrowful and troubled. 38 Then he said to them, "My soul is very sorrowful, even to death; remain here, and watch with me." 39 And going a little farther he fell on his face and prayed, "My Father, if it be possible, let this cup pass from me; nevertheless, not as I will, but as thou wilt." 40 And he came to the disciples and found them sleeping; and he said to Peter, "So, could you not watch with me one hour? 41 Watch and pray that you may not enter into temptation; the spirit indeed is willing, but the flesh is weak." 42 Again, for the second time, he went away and prayed, "My Father, if this cannot pass unless I drink it, thy will be done." 43 And again he came and found them sleeping, for their eyes were heavy. 44 So, leaving them again, he went away and prayed for the third time, saying the same words. 45 Then he came to the disciples and said to them, "Are you still sleeping and taking your rest? Behold, the hour is at hand, and the Son of man is betrayed into the hands of sinners. 46 Rise, let us be going; see, my betrayer is at hand."

Reflection: Jesus was suffering greatly in the Garden of Gethsemane. He saw clearly what he was about to undergo in his passion and death. He prayed to God his Father, "My Father, if it be possible, let this cup pass from me; nevertheless, not as I will, but as thou wilt." This is a beautiful lesson on how to pray during our suffering and to offer up our sufferings as Jesus did. "We know that in everything God works for good with those who love him, who are called according to his purpose." (Romans 8:28)

"The Scourging at the Pillar," a stained glass window, Saint Patrick Church, Lowell, MA

Bible Story: After Jesus prayed in the Garden of Gethsemane, a crowd came with swords and clubs and arrested him. They took him to the high priest and they asked if he was the Messiah, the Son of God. Jesus said that he was. The chief priests and elders didn't believe him and accused him of blasphemy (being disrespectful to God or claiming to be God). In the morning, they handed him over to the Roman ruler, Pontius Pilate. Pilate asked Jesus if he were the "King of the Jews." Jesus said that his Kingdom was not of this world. Pilate didn't want to be responsible for putting Jesus to death, so he let the crowd decide and they shouted to crucify Jesus. Pilate had Jesus cruelly whipped.

Reflection: Jesus' suffering shows us how terrible sin is in God's eyes for Jesus to have to undergo such suffering to make up for it. Jesus suffered for us. Will we accept the Lord Jesus as our Lord and stop sinning?

Bible Reading:

John 18:28-40, 19:1

28 Then they led Jesus from the house of Caiaphas to the praetorium. It was early. They themselves did not enter the praetorium, so that they might not be defiled, but might eat the passover. 29 So Pilate went out to them and said, "What accusation do you bring against this man?" 30 They answered him, "If this man were not an evildoer, we would not have handed him over." 31 Pilate said to them, "Take him yourselves and judge him by your own law." The Jews said to him, "It is not lawful for us to put any man to death." 32 This was to fulfil the word which Jesus had spoken to show by what death he was to die. 33 Pilate entered the praetorium again and called Jesus, and said to him, "Are you the King of the Jews?" 34 Jesus answered, "Do you say this of your own accord, or did others say it to you about me?" 35 Pilate answered, "Am I a Jew? Your own nation and the chief priests have handed you over to me; what have you done?" 36 Jesus answered, "My kingship is not of this world; if my kingship were of this world, my servants would fight, that I might not be handed over to the Jews; but my kingship is not from the world." 37 Pilate said to him, "So you are a king?" Jesus answered, "You say that I am a king. For this I was born, and for this I have come into the world, to bear witness to the truth. Every one who is of the truth hears my voice." 38 Pilate said to him, "What is truth?" After he had said this, he went out to the Jews again, and told them, "I find no crime in him. 39 But you have a custom that I should release one man for you at the Passover; will you have me release for you the King of the Jews?" 40 They cried out again, "Not this man, but Barabbas!" Now Barabbas was a robber....19:1 Then Pilate took Jesus and scourged him.

Ecce Homo (Behold, the Man!)
by Bartolome Esteban Murrillo, circa 1675

Bible Story: After Jesus was whipped and scourged, so that he was bleeding all over, they made fun of him. They took off his clothes and put on a royal purple cloak and made a crown of thorns to put on his head. They saluted him and said, "Hail, King of the Jews!" They struck his head with a stick to torture him. They spat on him and knelt down to pretend to do him homage. Pilate brought Jesus out before the crowd again in the purple cloak and said, "Behold the Man!" (John 19:5) Pilate said that he found no fault in Jesus, but the crowd shouted, "Crucify him."

Reflection: People can be cruel sometimes. They made fun of Jesus and tortured him, but he prayed for them in return. God is all good and loves everyone including sinners. Jesus said to bless those who curse you and to return good for evil. Do you do this in your life?

Bible Reading:

Mark 15:1-20

¹ And as soon as it was morning the chief priests, with the elders and scribes, and the whole council held a consultation; and they bound Jesus and led him away and delivered him to Pilate. ² And Pilate asked him, "Are you the King of the Jews?" And he answered him, "You have said so." ³ And the chief priests accused him of many things. ⁴ And Pilate again asked him, "Have you no answer to make? See how many charges they bring against you." ⁵ But Jesus made no further answer, so that Pilate wondered. ⁶ Now at the feast he used to release for them one prisoner for whom they asked. ⁷ And among the rebels in prison, who had committed murder in the insurrection, there was a man called Barabbas. ⁸ And the crowd came up and began to ask Pilate to do as he was wont to do for them. ⁹ And he answered them, "Do you want me to release for you the King of the Jews?" ¹⁰ For he perceived that it was out of envy that the chief priests had delivered him up. ¹¹ But the chief priests stirred up the crowd to have him release for them Barabbas instead. ¹² And Pilate again said to them, "Then what shall I do with the man whom you call the King of the Jews?" ¹³ And they cried out again, "Crucify him." ¹⁴ And Pilate said to them, "Why, what evil has he done?" But they shouted all the more, "Crucify him." ¹⁵ So Pilate, wishing to satisfy the crowd, released for them Barabbas; and having scourged Jesus, he delivered him to be crucified. ¹⁶ And the soldiers led him away inside the palace (that is, the praetorium); and they called together the whole battalion. ¹⁷ And they clothed him in a purple cloak, and plaiting a crown of thorns they put it on him. ¹⁸ And they began to salute him, "Hail, King of the Jews!" ¹⁹ And they struck his head with a reed, and spat upon him, and they knelt down in homage to him. ²⁰ And when they had mocked him, they stripped him of the purple cloak, and put his own clothes on him. And they led him out to crucify him.

The Fourth Sorrowful Mystery
The Carrying of the Cross

Christ Carrying the Cross by Eustache Le Sueur, 1617-1655

Reflection: Like Jesus, we all have crosses in our lives. Jesus said, "If any man would come after me, let him deny himself and take up his cross daily and follow me." (Luke 9:23)
Have you decided to follow Jesus? Do you offer up your sufferings for the conversion of sinners and salvation of souls?

Bible Story: Jesus was led away to be crucified and was made to carry his cross. At one point the soldiers made Simon of Cyrene help carry the cross. People were following Jesus, and women were crying for him. He told the women not to weep for him, but to weep for themselves and for their children. According to tradition, one of the women was Veronica. She wiped Jesus' face with her veil and a miracle took place in that a picture of Jesus' face was left on her veil.

Bible Reading:

 Luke 23:13-16, 18-32

¹³ Pilate then called together the chief priests and the rulers and the people, ¹⁴ and said to them, "You brought me this man as one who was perverting the people; and after examining him before you, behold, I did not find this man guilty of any of your charges against him; ¹⁵ neither did Herod, for he sent him back to us. Behold, nothing deserving death has been done by him; ¹⁶ I will therefore chastise him and release him."... ¹⁸ But they all cried out together, "Away with this man, and release to us Barabbas" -- ¹⁹ a man who had been thrown into prison for an insurrection started in the city, and for murder. ²⁰ Pilate addressed them once more, desiring to release Jesus; ²¹ but they shouted out, "Crucify, crucify him!" ²² A third time he said to them, "Why, what evil has he done? I have found in him no crime deserving death; I will therefore chastise him and release him." ²³ But they were urgent, demanding with loud cries that he should be crucified. And their voices prevailed. ²⁴ So Pilate gave sentence that their demand should be granted. ²⁵ He released the man who had been thrown into prison for insurrection and murder, whom they asked for; but Jesus he delivered up to their will. ²⁶ And as they led him away, they seized one Simon of Cyrene, who was coming in from the country, and laid on him the cross, to carry it behind Jesus. ²⁷ And there followed him a great multitude of the people, and of women who bewailed and lamented him. ²⁸ But Jesus turning to them said, "Daughters of Jerusalem, do not weep for me, but weep for yourselves and for your children. ²⁹ For behold, the days are coming when they will say, `Blessed are the barren, and the wombs that never bore, and the breasts that never gave suck!' ³⁰ Then they will begin to say to the mountains, `Fall on us'; and to the hills, `Cover us.' ³¹ For if they do this when the wood is green, what will happen when it is dry?" ³² Two others also, who were criminals, were led away to be put to death with him.

Crucifixion, 19th Century artist

Bible Story: When they arrived at Mt. Calvary, they stripped Jesus of his clothes and nailed him to the cross. Jesus was offered wine mixed with gall to drink. He was then crucified and hung on the cross between two convicted thieves. According to Mark's Gospel, Jesus hung on the cross for about six hours from 9:00 in the morning until his death at about 3:00 in the afternoon. The soldiers put a sign on the cross above his head which said, "Jesus of Nazareth, King of the Jews" in three languages. (John 19:20) They divided his garments and cast lots for his robe. The soldiers did not break Jesus' legs, as they did to the other two crucified men. A soldier thrust a lance into his side, and blood and water flowed out showing that Jesus was dead. Then they buried him.

Bible Reading:

Luke 23:33-49

33 And when they came to the place which is called The Skull, there they crucified him, and the criminals, one on the right and one on the left. 34 And Jesus said, "Father, forgive them; for they know not what they do." And they cast lots to divide his garments. 35 And the people stood by, watching; but the rulers scoffed at him, saying, "He saved others; let him save himself, if he is the Christ of God, his Chosen One!" 36 The soldiers also mocked him, coming up and offering him vinegar, 37 and saying, "If you are the King of the Jews, save yourself!" 38 There was also an inscription over him, "This is the King of the Jews." 39 One of the criminals who were hanged railed at him, saying, "Are you not the Christ? Save yourself and us!" 40 But the other rebuked him, saying, "Do you not fear God, since you are under the same sentence of condemnation? 41 And we indeed justly; for we are receiving the due reward of our deeds; but this man has done nothing wrong." 42 And he said, "Jesus, remember me when you come into your kingdom." 43 And he said to him, "Truly, I say to you, today you will be with me in Paradise." 44 It was now about the sixth hour, and there was darkness over the whole land until the ninth hour, 45 while the sun's light failed; and the curtain of the temple was torn in two. 46 Then Jesus, crying with a loud voice, said, "Father, into thy hands I commit my spirit!" And having said this he breathed his last. 47 Now when the centurion saw what had taken place, he praised God, and said, "Certainly this man was innocent!" 48 And all the multitudes who assembled to see the sight, when they saw what had taken place, returned home beating their breasts. 49 And all his acquaintances and the women who had followed him from Galilee stood at a distance and saw these things.

Reflection: Jesus offered himself as a sacrifice for sin to make it possible for us to go to heaven someday. No matter how great our sins, Jesus' mercy is greater. Jesus loves us, died for us, and wants to forgive us. He is a greater Savior than we are a sinner. Jesus greatly desires that we trust in his mercy. (www.divinemercy.org)

1st Glorious Mystery: The Resurrection

Resurrection, Carl Heinrich Bloch, 1873

Bible Story: After Jesus died on the cross on Good Friday, his body was wrapped in a linen cloth and buried in a tomb. On the third day, Easter Sunday, he rose from the dead, which means his body came back to life. Mary Magdalene and the other Mary went to visit the tomb. They found the stone rolled back and Jesus' body was missing. They saw an angel, and later Jesus appeared to them and said to tell the apostles all they had seen. Jesus also appeared many times to the apostles and others.

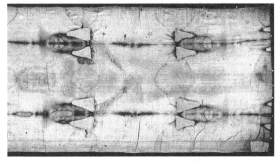

The Shroud of Turin is thought to be the burial cloth of Jesus. Many scientific studies have been done on the image including one by the STURP team of American scientists. They found no reliable evidence of forgery, and said it was "a mystery" as to how the image was formed. (www.shroud.com)

Bible Reading:

 Matthew 28:1-10, 16-20

1 Now after the sabbath, toward the dawn of the first day of the week, Mary Magdalene and the other Mary went to see the sepulchre. 2 And behold, there was a great earthquake; for an angel of the Lord descended from heaven and came and rolled back the stone, and sat upon it. 3 His appearance was like lightning, and his raiment white as snow. 4 And for fear of him the guards trembled and became like dead men. 5 But the angel said to the women, "Do not be afraid; for I know that you seek Jesus who was crucified. 6 He is not here; for he has risen, as he said. Come, see the place where he lay. 7 Then go quickly and tell his disciples that he has risen from the dead, and behold, he is going before you to Galilee; there you will see him. Lo, I have told you." 8 So they departed quickly from the tomb with fear and great joy, and ran to tell his disciples. 9 And behold, Jesus met them and said, "Hail!" And they came up and took hold of his feet and worshiped him. 10 Then Jesus said to them, "Do not be afraid; go and tell my brethren to go to Galilee, and there they will see me."... 16 Now the eleven disciples went to Galilee, to the mountain to which Jesus had directed them. 17 And when they saw him they worshiped him; but some doubted. 18 And Jesus came and said to them, "All authority in heaven and on earth has been given to me. 19 Go therefore and make disciples of all nations, baptizing them in the name of the Father and of the Son and of the Holy Spirit, 20 teaching them to observe all that I have commanded you; and lo, I am with you always, to the close of the age."

Reflection: Just as Jesus' body rose from the dead, after we die our own bodies will also be resurrected on the last day, and "...and these whom He justified, He also glorified." (Rom. 8:30) Who will separate us from the love of Christ? (Rom. 8:35)

Ascension of Jesus, ceiling-painting in parish church in Spittal an der Drau 3, Austria

Bible Reading:

Acts 1:1-11

1 In the first book, O Theophilus, I have dealt with all that Jesus began to do and teach, 2 until the day when he was taken up, after he had given commandment through the Holy Spirit to the apostles whom he had chosen. 3 To them he presented himself alive after his passion by many proofs, appearing to them during forty days, and speaking of the kingdom of God. 4 And while staying with them he charged them not to depart from Jerusalem, but to wait for the promise of the Father, which, he said, "you heard from me, 5 for John baptized with water, but before many days you shall be baptized with the Holy Spirit." 6 So when they had come together, they asked him, "Lord, will you at this time restore the kingdom to Israel?" 7 He said to them, "It is not for you to know times or seasons which the Father has fixed by his own authority. 8 But you shall receive power when the Holy Spirit has come upon you; and you shall be my witnesses in Jerusalem and in all Judea and Samaria and to the end of the earth." 9 And when he had said this, as they were looking on, he was lifted up, and a cloud took him out of their sight. 10 And while they were gazing into heaven as he went, behold, two men stood by them in white robes, 11 and said, "Men of Galilee, why do you stand looking into heaven? This Jesus, who was taken up from you into heaven, will come in the same way as you saw him go into heaven."

Bible Story: One evening after Jesus rose from the dead, he appeared to the disciples and said, "Peace be with you." He showed them his hands, feet, and side. The disciples were very happy to see him and rejoiced. Jesus said to them, "As the Father has sent me, even so I send you." He breathed on them and said, "Receive the Holy Spirit. If you forgive the sins of any, they are forgiven; if you retain the sins of any, they are retained." (from John 20:19-23). Jesus appeared many other times and performed many other signs as well. One day, he told the apostles that they would be baptized with the Holy Spirit in a few days. Then Jesus was lifted up in a cloud and went to heaven. Two men with white robes told the disciples that Jesus will come again from heaven on a cloud. This is called the Second Coming and will happen at the end of the world.

Reflection: With Jesus' death, his suffering ended and ours will too if we follow Jesus. "And when I go and prepare a place for you, I will come again and will take you to myself, that where I am you may be also." (John 14:3) "But, as it is written, 'What no eye has seen, nor ear heard, nor the heart of man conceived, what God has prepared for those who love him.'" (1 Cor. 2:9) Have you decided to be a follower of Jesus?

The Second Glorious Mystery
The Ascension

Bible Story: After Jesus went up into heaven, the apostles went back to Jerusalem and spent their time in prayer. When the day of Pentecost came they were all gathered in one place. All of a sudden from the sky came a loud noise like a strong wind which they all heard. Tongues as of fire came to rest on each of them, and they were all filled with the Holy Spirit. Many people from various places were in Jerusalem that day, and the apostles proclaimed to them about what God has done through Jesus, the Messiah. They heard them in their own languages and asked what they needed to do. Peter said, "Repent and be baptized...in the name of Jesus Christ that your sins may be forgiven; then you shall receive the gift of the Holy Spirit." (Acts 2:38) About 3,000 people were baptized that day. Pentecost is sometimes called the "Birthday of the Church."

Pentecost by El Greco, 1600s

Bible Reading:

Acts 2:1-18

1 When the day of Pentecost had come, they were all together in one place. 2 And suddenly a sound came from heaven like the rush of a mighty wind, and it filled all the house where they were sitting. 3 And there appeared to them tongues as of fire, distributed and resting on each one of them. 4 And they were all filled with the Holy Spirit and began to speak in other tongues, as the Spirit gave them utterance. 5 Now there were dwelling in Jerusalem Jews, devout men from every nation under heaven. 6 And at this sound the multitude came together, and they were bewildered, because each one heard them speaking in his own language. 7 And they were amazed and wondered, saying, "Are not all these who are speaking Galileans? 8 And how is it that we hear, each of us in his own native language? 9 Parthians and Medes and Elamites and residents of Mesopotamia, Judea and Cappadocia, Pontus and Asia, 10 Phrygia and Pamphylia, Egypt and the parts of Libya belonging to Cyrene, and visitors from Rome, both Jews and proselytes, 11 Cretans and Arabians, we hear them telling in our own tongues the mighty works of God." 12 And all were amazed and perplexed, saying to one another, "What does this mean?" 13 But others mocking said, "They are filled with new wine." 14 But Peter, standing with the eleven, lifted up his voice and addressed them, "Men of Judea and all who dwell in Jerusalem, let this be known to you, and give ear to my words. 15 For these men are not drunk, as you suppose, since it is only the third hour of the day; 16 but this is what was spoken by the prophet Joel: 17 'And in the last days it shall be, God declares, that I will pour out my Spirit upon all flesh, and your sons and your daughters shall prophesy, and your young men shall see visions, and your old men shall dream dreams; 18 yea, and on my menservants and my maidservants in those days I will pour out my Spirit; and they shall prophesy.

Reflection: "...Confirmation is the special outpouring of the Holy Spirit as once granted to the apostles on the day of Pentecost." *Catechism of the Catholic Church* #1302. The promise is for all "whom the Lord our God calls to him." (Act 2:39) Are you answering God's call?

The Assumption of the Virgin by
Bartolomé Esteban Murillo, 1670s

Mary was honored by God to be the mother of Jesus. God created her without the stain of Original Sin on her soul because she was going to be the mother of Jesus. She lived a very holy life doing all that God asked her. When it was time for Mary to die, Mary's body and soul were taken up to heaven to be with God. Based on the tradition of the church in 1950, Pius XII infallibly defined the Assumption of Mary as a dogma of faith: "We pronounce, declare and define it to be a divinely revealed dogma that the immaculate Mother of God, the ever Virgin Mary, having completed the course of her earthly life, was assumed body and soul to heavenly glory."

Defining the Dogma of the Assumption, Munificentissimus Deus, Apostolic Constitution of Pope Pius XII issued November 1, 1950

Catholic Teachings:

Catechism of the Catholic Church #966:
"'Finally the Immaculate Virgin, preserved free from all stain of original sin, when the course of her earthly life was finished, was taken up body and soul into heavenly glory, and exalted by the Lord as Queen over all things, so that she might be the more fully conformed to her Son, the Lord of lords and conqueror of sin and death.'¹ The Assumption of the Blessed Virgin is a singular participation in her Son's Resurrection and an anticipation of the resurrection of other Christians." ¹*LG* 59; cf. Pius XII, *Munificentissimus Deus* (1950): DS 3903; cf. *Rev* 19:16.

"Just as the Mother of Jesus, glorified in body and soul in heaven, is the image and beginning of the Church as it is to be perfected in the world to come, so too does she shine forth on earth, until the day of the Lord shall come, (cf. 2 Pet. 3:10) as a sign of sure hope and solace to the people of God during its sojourn on earth." *From Vatican II, Dogmatic Constitution on the Church, (68) 75*

Bible Reading:

1 Corinthians 15:13-18

¹³ But if there is no resurrection of the dead, then Christ has not been raised; ¹⁴ if Christ has not been raised, then our preaching is in vain and your faith is in vain. ¹⁵ We are even found to be misrepresenting God, because we testified of God that he raised Christ, whom he did not raise if it is true that the dead are not raised. ¹⁶ For if the dead are not raised, then Christ has not been raised. ¹⁷ If Christ has not been raised, your faith is futile and you are still in your sins. ¹⁸ Then those also who have fallen asleep in Christ have perished.

Reflection: The Bible and the Catholic Church teach that we are to worship God alone and to love God above all things. (We are not to worship anyone or anything else besides God.) Also, we are following Jesus' example if we love and honor Mary and the Saints. In prayer, we can ask Mary and the Saints in heaven to pray for us just as we ask our friends to pray for us. Do you ask Mary and the Saints to pray for you?

The Fourth Glorious Mystery
The Assumption

The Fifth Glorious Mystery
The Coronation of Mary

The Coronation of the Virgin
by Diego Velázquez, 1641-1644

Mary is crowned in heaven with the glory of a Queen. She is a Queen because she is the mother of Jesus, who is called a King because he is our Savior and the Son of God. She is not only a Queen, but since we are children of God, she is also our mother in heaven who loves us very much and prays for us.

Bible Reading: Luke 1:46-49

[46] And Mary said, "My soul magnifies the Lord, [47] and my spirit rejoices in God my Savior, [48] for he has regarded the low estate of his handmaiden. For behold, henceforth all generations will call me blessed; [49] for he who is mighty has done great things for me, and holy is his name."

Ad Caeli Reginam: Encyclical of Pope Pius XII on Proclaiming the Queenship of Mary

"From the earliest ages of the catholic church a Christian people, whether in time of triumph or more especially in time of crisis, has addressed prayers of petition and hymns of praise and veneration to the Queen of heaven. And never has that hope wavered which they placed in the Mother of the Divine King, Jesus Christ; nor has that faith ever failed by which we are taught that Mary, the Virgin Mother of God, reigns with a mother's solicitude over the entire world, just as she is crowned in heavenly blessedness with the glory of a Queen.... 38. From these considerations, the proof develops on these lines: if Mary, in taking an active part in the work of salvation, was, by God's design, associated with Jesus Christ, the source of salvation itself, in a manner comparable to that in which Eve was associated with Adam, the source of death, so that it may be stated that the work of our salvation was accomplished by a kind of 'recapitulation,' in which a virgin was instrumental in the salvation of the human race, just as a virgin had been closely associated with its death; if, moreover, it can likewise be stated that this glorious Lady had been chosen Mother of Christ 'in order that she might become a partner in the redemption of the human race'; and if, in truth, 'it was she who, free of the stain of actual and original sin, and ever most closely bound to her Son, on Golgotha offered that Son to the Eternal Father together with the complete sacrifice of her maternal rights and maternal love, like a new Eve, for all the sons of Adam, stained as they were by his lamentable fall,' then it may be legitimately concluded that as Christ, the new Adam, must be called a King not merely because He is Son of God, but also because He is our Redeemer, so, analogously, the Most Blessed Virgin is queen not only because she is Mother of God, but also because, as the new Eve, she was associated with the new Adam."

Reflection: Mary is an example of how to worship, love, and follow Jesus, and Jesus is an example of how to love and honor Mary. Jesus and Mary love you. Do you love Jesus? Do you love Mary as Jesus did and as your mother in heaven? Do you follow the example Jesus and Mary set for us?

Our Lady of Fatima is a name given to the Blessed Virgin Mary. She appeared to three children, Lucia dos Santos and her cousins, Jacinta and Francisco Marto, in Fatima, Portugal in 1917 on the 13th day of six months in a row starting on May 13. Mary told the children many things including to pray the rosary daily to obtain peace in the world and to offer sacrifices for the conversion of sinners. Mary also predicted future events that came true and gave the children three secrets which they could tell later.

The seers of Fatima:
Lúcia Santos (left)
with her cousins
Francisco and Jacinta
Marto, 1917

Apparitions of the Angel in 1916

Before Mary appeared to the children, an angel appeared to them three times in 1916. The first time they were tending their sheep and a strong wind shook the trees. Startled, the children looked up to see a figure coming towards them above the trees. Lucia said, "It was a young man, about fourteen or fifteen years old, whiter than snow, transparent as crystal when the sun shines through it, and of great beauty. On reaching us, he said: 'Do not be afraid! I am the Angel of Peace. Pray with me.' Kneeling on the ground, he bowed down until his forehead touched the ground, and made us repeat these words three times: 'My God, I believe, I adore, I hope and I love You! I ask pardon of You for those who do not believe, do not adore, do not hope and do not love You.' "*

At the second appearance the Angel said, "Pray, pray very much! The most holy Hearts of Jesus and Mary have designs of mercy on you. Offer prayers and sacrifices constantly to the Most High...Make of everything you can a sacrifice, and offer it to God as an act of reparation for the sins by which He is offended, and in supplication for the conversion of sinners. You will thus draw down peace upon your country. I am its Angel Guardian, the Angel of Portugal. Above all, accept and bear with submission, the suffering which the Lord will send you."*

Another time while tending their sheep the Angel appeared again. Lucia said the Angel was "holding a chalice in his left hand, with the Host suspended above it, from which some drops of blood fell into the chalice... The Angel knelt down beside us and made us repeat three times: 'Most Holy Trinity, Father, Son and Holy Spirit, I adore You profoundly, and I offer You the most precious Body, Blood, Soul and Divinity of Jesus Christ, present in all the tabernacles of the world, in reparation for the outrages, sacrileges and indifference with which He Himself is offended. And, through the infinite merits of His most Sacred Heart, and the Immaculate Heart of Mary, I beg of You the conversion of poor sinners.' "*

Apparitions of Mary in 1917

On May 13, 1917, ten-year-old Lucia and her younger cousins Jacinta and Francisco were tending sheep at the Cova da Iria near their home village of Fatima, Portugal. Lucia saw a woman "more brilliant than the sun, and radiated a light more clear and intense than a crystal glass filled with sparkling water, when the rays of the burning sun shine through it."* Mary asked the children to do penance and "acts of reparation, and to make sacrifices to save sinners." (Sinners are people who through their own free choice disobey God by doing what they know is wrong, or by not doing what something they know they should do.) The conversion of sinners means to amend or change one's life according to the teachings of Jesus. Mary told the children that more souls go to hell for unrepented sins of impurity than for any other reason. She also said that certain styles and fashions were being introduced which gravely offend Jesus. This means we need to dress modestly so as not to be the occasion of sin to others.

The Blessed Mother said to the children, "Sacrifice yourselves for sinners, and say many times to Jesus, especially whenever you make some sacrifice: O Jesus, it is for love of You, for the conversion of sinners, and in reparation for the sins committed against the Immaculate Heart of Mary."*

> Our Lady of Fatima said, "Pray the Rosary every day, in order to obtain peace for the world, and the end of the war."*

On one occasion, Lucia asked Mary if she would take them to heaven. Mary said, "Yes. I will take Jacinta and Francisco soon. But you are to stay here some time longer. Jesus wishes to make use of you to make me known and loved. He wants to establish in the world devotion to my Immaculate Heart."* This prophecy later came true as both Francisco and Jacinta died of the Spanish flu while still children, but Lucia became a nun and lived to be 97 years old.

When people heard about the visions and miracles at Fatima, thousands of people came to see for themselves. On August 13, 1917, the government administrator, who didn't believe in the Catholic religion and did not like all the people coming to Fatima, put the children in jail. The administrator questioned the children and tried to get them to tell the three secrets Mary had told them not to tell yet. The children refused even though he said he would boil them in oil if they did not tell him the secrets. The children were aged 10, 9, and 7 at the time.

The Miracle of the Sun

Mary promised a miracle would occur in October so that all may believe. About 70,000 people came that day to see the miracle including newspaper reporters and photographers. All of a sudden, Lucia called out to the crowd to look at the sun. People saw the sun appearing to change colors and rotate like a wheel and some thought the sun was falling to the earth. Some thought it was the end of the world. Even some people in nearby towns saw the miracle.

Photograph taken during the "Dance of the Sun" at Fatima on October 13, 1917.

Reports of the Miracle of the Sun

O Século (a pro-government, anti-clerical, Lisbon newspaper), reported the following: "Before the astonished eyes of the crowd, whose aspect was biblical as they stood bareheaded, eagerly searching the sky, the sun trembled, made sudden incredible movements outside all cosmic laws---the sun 'danced' according to the typical expression of the people."

An eye witness report in the newspaper Ordem said, "The sun, at one moment surrounded with scarlet flame, at another aureoled in yellow and deep purple, seemed to be in an exceedingly fast and whirling movement, at times appearing to be loosened from the sky and to be approaching the earth, strongly radiating heat."

The October 17, 1917 edition of the Lisbon daily, O Dia, reported the following, "At one o'clock in the afternoon, midday by the sun, the rain stopped. The sky, pearly grey in colour, illuminated the vast arid landscape with a strange light. The sun had a transparent gauzy veil so that the eyes could easily be fixed upon it. The grey mother-of-pearl tone turned into a sheet of silver which broke up as the clouds were torn apart and the silver sun, enveloped in the same gauzy grey light, was seen to whirl and turn in the circle of broken clouds. A cry went up from every mouth and people fell on their knees on the muddy ground.... The light turned a beautiful blue, as if it had come through the stained-glass windows of a cathedral, and spread itself over the people who knelt with outstretched hands. The blue faded slowly, and then the light seemed to pass through yellow glass. Yellow stains fell against white handkerchiefs, against the dark skirts of the women. They were repeated on the trees, on the stones and on the serra. People wept and prayed with uncovered heads, in the presence of a miracle they had awaited. The seconds seemed like hours, so vivid were they."

The above quotes about the miracle are from www.ewtn.com/fatima/apparitions/October.htm.

A photograph of the crowd taken during the miracle at Fatima on October 13, 1917.

The Secret of Fatima (Three Parts)

The first part of the secret was a vision of hell, which Lucia describes as follows: "Well, the secret is made up of three distinct parts, two of which I am now going to reveal. The first part is the vision of hell. Our Lady showed us a great sea of fire which seemed to be under the earth. Plunged in this fire were demons and souls in human form, like transparent burning embers, all blackened or burnished bronze, floating about in the conflagration, now

raised into the air by the flames that issued from within themselves together with great clouds of smoke, now falling back on every side like sparks in a huge fire, without weight or equilibrium, and amid shrieks and groans of pain and despair, which horrified us and made us tremble with fear. The demons could be distinguished by their terrifying and repulsive likeness to frightful and unknown animals, all black and transparent. This vision lasted but an instant. How can we ever be grateful enough to our kind heavenly Mother, who had already prepared us by promising, in the first Apparition, to take us to heaven. Otherwise, I think we would have died of fear and terror."*

The second part of the secret included Mary's instructions on how to save souls from hell and convert the world to the Christian faith. Lucia said in her Third Memoir: "We then looked up at Our Lady, who said to us so kindly and so sadly: "You have seen hell where the souls of poor sinners go. To save them, God wishes to establish in the world devotion to my Immaculate Heart. If what I say to you is done, many souls will be saved and there will be peace. The war is going to end: but if people do not cease offending God, a worse one will break out during the Pontificate of Pius XI. When you see a night illumined by an unknown light, know that this is the great sign given you by God that he is about to punish the world for its crimes, by means of war, famine, and persecutions of the Church and of the Holy Father. To prevent this, I shall come to ask for the consecration of Russia to my Immaculate Heart, and the Communion of reparation on the First Saturdays. If my requests are heeded, Russia will be converted, and there will be peace; if not, she will spread her errors throughout the world, causing wars and persecutions of the Church. The good will be martyred; the Holy Father will have much to suffer; various nations will be annihilated. In the end, my Immaculate Heart will triumph. The Holy Father will consecrate Russia to me, and she shall be converted, and a period of peace will be granted to the world."*

This all happened as Mary said as people did not do what was needed. In Russia the Communists took over. They killed millions of people and took over other countries. They took away many freedoms such as the freedom of religion and the freedom of speech, and sometimes personal property.

"**The third part of the secret** revealed at the Cova da Iria-Fatima, on 13 July 1917. I write in obedience to you, my God, who command me to do so through his Excellency the Bishop of Leiria and through your Most Holy Mother and mine. After the two parts which I have already explained, at the left of Our Lady and a little above, we saw an Angel with a flaming sword in his left hand; flashing, it gave out flames that looked as though they would set the world on fire; but they died out in contact with the splendour that Our Lady radiated towards him from her right hand: pointing to the earth with his right hand, the Angel cried out in a loud voice: 'Penance, Penance, Penance!' And we saw in an immense light that is God: 'something similar to how people appear in a mirror when they pass in front of it' a Bishop dressed in White 'we had the impression that it was the Holy Father'. Other Bishops, Priests, men and women Religious going up a steep mountain, at the top of which there was a big Cross of rough-hewn trunks as of a cork-tree with the bark; before reaching there the Holy Father passed through a big city half in ruins and half trembling with halting step, afflicted with pain and sorrow, he prayed for the souls of the corpses he met on his way; having reached the top of the mountain, on his knees at the foot of the big Cross he was killed by a group of soldiers who fired bullets and arrows at him, and in the same way there died one after another the other Bishops, Priests, men and women Religious, and various lay people of different ranks and positions. Beneath the two arms of the Cross there were two Angels each with a crystal aspersorium in his hand, in which they gathered up the blood of the Martyrs and with it sprinkled the souls that were making their way to God. - *Tuy-3-1-1944*"*

Lucia Santos (age 10, in the middle) and her two cousins: Francisco (age 9) and Jacinta Marto (age 7) holding their rosaries. Fatima, Portugal.

Official Position of the Church

Private revelations are not part of the deposit of faith of the Catholic Church, and we do not have to believe in them, but the church investigated the apparitions at Fatima and judged them "worthy of belief." Also the Church is in the process of declaring Lucia, Francisco, and Jacinta Saints. Francisco and Jacinta have been beatified, and they are now called Blessed Francisco and Blessed Jacinta. Jacinta is said to be the youngest nonmartyred person to ever be beatified and may some day be the youngest nonmartyred canonized Saint.

Fatima: Reaffirmation of the Gospel

Overall, the Fatima message reaffirms many teachings of the Catholic faith and the reality of the supernatural realm which is denied by atheists and materialists such as the Gospel message of Jesus, prayer, sin, heaven, hell, angels, miracles, and the Eucharist as the body, blood, soul and divinity of Jesus. It also encourages devotion to Mary who told us how to help save sinners, how to prevent wars, and how to bring peace into the world by obeying Jesus, offering sacrifices, and praying the rosary.

*Quotations marked with an asterisk (*) are from the PDF version of *Fatima in Lucia's Own Words* at www.catholic-soe.org/catholicbooks.html. Another recommended ebook at the same website is *Calls by Sister Lucia*. Both are free to download.

Jesus Blessing the Children,
Bernhard Plockhorst, 1805-1907

Bible Reading:

Mark 9:35-37

³⁵ And he sat down and called the twelve; and he said to them, "If any one would be first, he must be last of all and servant of all." ³⁶ And he took a child, and put him in the midst of them; and taking him in his arms, he said to them, ³⁷ "Whoever receives one such child in my name receives me; and whoever receives me, receives not me but him who sent me."

Mark 10:13-16

¹³ And they were bringing children to him, that he might touch them; and the disciples rebuked them. ¹⁴ But when Jesus saw it he was indignant, and said to them, "Let the children come to me, do not hinder them; for to such belongs the kingdom of God. ¹⁵ Truly, I say to you, whoever does not receive the kingdom of God like a child shall not enter it." ¹⁶ And he took them in his arms and blessed them, laying his hands upon them.

Bible Story: Jesus loves all the people in the world, and he especially loves children. One day Jesus was teaching a crowd of people how to live and obey God's laws. There were families in the crowd who had children, and they brought their children up to Jesus hoping that he might bless them. The disciples scolded them and tried to send the children away, but Jesus told them that he wanted them to let the children come to him. He took the children in his arms and blessed them. He told the people they must become like children to enter the kingdom of heaven, and that the greatest in the kingdom of heaven is humble like a little child.

Reflection: "At that time the disciples came to Jesus, saying, 'Who is the greatest in the kingdom of heaven?' And calling to him a child, he put him in the midst of them, and said, 'Truly, I say to you, unless you turn and become like children, you will never enter the kingdom of heaven. Whoever humbles himself like this child, he is the greatest in the kingdom of heaven.'" (Matthew 18:1-4) Do you humble yourself like a child before God? Do you believe, trust, love, and obey God? Do you pray? To know and understand what God wants, do you study the Bible and the teachings of the Church such as the *Catechism of the Catholic Church*? Do you accept Jesus as your Lord and Savior? If not, why not decide today to be a follower of Jesus Christ?

Jesus Blesses the Children

"Let the children come to me, do not hinder them; for to such belongs the kingdom of God."
(Mark 10:14)

CPSIA information can be obtained at www.ICGtesting.com
Printed in the USA
LVOW01s2225030515

437071LV00004B/12/P